WORDS UNWHISPERED

Ghazals in the Time of the Pandemic, 2021

Pamela L. Laskin

Červená Barva Press
Somerville, Massachusetts

Copyright © 2023

All rights reserved. No part of this book may be reproduced in any manner without written consent except for the quotation of short passages used inside of an article, criticism, or review.

Červená Barva Press

P.O. Box 440357

W. Somerville, MA 02144

www.cervenabarvapress.com

Bookstore: www.thelostbookshelf.com

Production: Allison O'Keefe

Cover Art: Elissa Cohen

ISBN: 978-1-950063-97-0

Library of Congress Control Number: 2023940914

ACKNOWLEDGMENTS

Acknowledgment is made to the following publications in which these poems appeared or will soon be appearing:

He Called for Mama, Big City Lit, Spring, 2021

Shared Room, Mer Vox 18, Winter, 2020

A Mother's Lament; Cradle in my Arms; End of the Semester; Facetime with Ella; The World Shut Down Its Hugs; With no Vaccine, Home Planet News

Prayers, Jane's Walk, NY

Poetry Outreach, 2020, Poetry in Performance 48

CONTENTS

Prayers	3
Coronavirus, 2020	4
Age	5
Alone	6
Unsorrowed	7
The Body	8
Blankets	9
Exiting the Shadows	10
Without a Breath	11
Hands of Grief	12
Grief	13
Food	14
Hunger	15
Sick	16
Hero	17
Covid, 2021	18
Sirens	19
What is Right?	20
The Gift of Ghazal	21
Life Preserver	22
Hidden	23
Cradle in my Arms	24
The World Shut Down Its Hugs	25
With No Vaccine	26
A Mother's Lament	27
He Called for Mama	28
Police Shootings June, 2020	29
Thriving	30
Rage	31
News of News	32
Facetime with Ella	33
Prayers 11: To Samantha Rose for her 30th	34
Shared Room: A ghazal	35
Verbal Gymnastics	36
Hands	37

Stuck Inside With You	38
My heart, my ghazal	39
Birthday Poem	40
End of the Semester	41
Back to School	42
The New Normal	43
Blind Black Box	44
Sighs and Cries	45
Election, 2020	46
The Virus Rages	47
Vaccine, 2021	48
Poetry Outreach, 2021	49

To Ira, Unstuck because of you!

WORDS UNWHISPERED

Ghazals in the Time of the Pandemic, 2021

Prayers

Writing was my talisman
it was my peace

now I dig for words
there is no peace

the world is Humpty Dumpty
shattered pieces

I try to search for dreams
in broken pieces

the virus bleeds us dry
there is no peace

but then I write this poem
my prayer for peace.

Coronavirus, 2020

The city has shut down
it is a plague,

my body undercover
sleeps in plague

my grief grows like a garden
of gangrened plagues

daily virus blooms
like any plague

the elderly are victims
they die in plagues

I try to stay inside
in hell I'm plagued

better than to die
and be the plague.

Age

An albatross of age
and I feel sick

the body moves like blisters
bursting, sick

cold weather cuts my fingers
arthritic, sick

the heat is not much better
sweating, sick

sorrow still in sunshine
sick, sick, sick.

Alone

No one walks the streets
which are alone,

frightened of the markets
one shops alone

playgrounds now are locked
swings, childless, alone

people wearing masks
they grieve, alone

thousands lie unburied
they die, alone.

Unsorrowed

Inside a bad dream
sorrow stuck on your skin

never at a loss for words
secrets shared of sorrow

often crackling laughter
walk away from sorrow

such different sisters
help me sail away from sorrow

we fight to stay together
discard excess skin, so sorrow

floats down the river
grows new skin, unsorrowed.

The Body

Searching for serenity
outside the body

sixty years still singing
a voice with body

the tunes are flat
in burdened body

since the world is sad
and every body

has to find release
from body's pain

dreams of desire
in body's stain.

Blankets

I'm chilled inside my bones
so need a blanket

sorrow saps my brain
is there a blanket?

I dream outside my body
draped in blankets

the trees bereft of leaves
they need a blanket

future without seas
there is no blanket

I seek to hide in you
inside your blanket.

Exiting the Shadows

Sorrow in my skin
I sleep in shadows

searching for an opening
inside the shadow

every step I take
a shadow follows

when I go to sleep
I dream of shadows

awakening to dawn
that's drenched in shadows

looking for an exit
from the shadow.

Without a Breath

My heart's unanchored in my chest
without a breath,

the world goes spinning wild
without a breath

oceans swallow sorrow
without a breath

deliberate tomorrow
without a breath

the morning still awakens
and has a breath

night eclipses star shine
a sigh, a breath.

Hands of Grief

The song I sing has lost its tune
replaced by sorrow

the trees are all bereft of leaves
they bend in sorrow

the sky is always winter blue
clouds float with sorrow

the dreams I had, now so few
aside from sorrow

I look upon your empty face
entrenched in sorrow

the body's casket cannot move
it's filled with sorrow.

Grief

The world is split in two
the grief is churning

this virus has me blue
the grief is churning

my boy, he stays so silent
the grief is churning

not sure where I can reach
when grief is churning

the future is unsure
when grief is churning

there is no open door
for grief that's churning.

Food

Begging on the streets
she needs some food

many stores are closed
shelves bare of food

crowds of jobless folks
rent-or food?

children who are hungry
for Mom, no food

months of hibernation
the same old food

and social isolation
no hugs, no food.

Hunger

The virus has a vise
it has much hunger,

it's killing people daily
with this hunger

the lungs are eaten up-
voracious hunger

and no one can deny
the grief of hunger

gaze at Mama's face
it's filled with hunger

how to feed her child
who cries of hunger.

Sick

Today she had a baby
and she got sick

her lungs became just liquid
that's how sick

the baby grasped her breasts
but she, too sick

hunger was a henchman
with Mama sick

and baby wanted Mama
such grief is sick

she'll never know this Mama
sick-sick-sick.

Hero

He is the Papa who wore a smile
at thirty-six, now dead

his little girl who had down syndrome
now her papa's dead

he once had dreams to own a store
at thirty-six, now dead

to find a Mama for his girl
at thirty-six, now dead

he coached a team in his spare time
at thirty-six, now dead

a hero, he, without a rhyme
at thirty-six, now dead.

Covid, 2021

My house is filled with fake plants
since they don't die

the leaves are green and radiant
they never die

I do not have to water them
they will not die

they think of me a botanist
they never die

with other shrubs my thumb is black
they always die

more than half a million dead
they all have died.

Sirens

The City is asleep
I hear a siren,

when the day awakens
the chimes of sirens

mid-day hear the cry
of sorrowed sirens,

open mouth of Munch
the scream of sirens

time to go to sleep
and still the sirens

daily dozens die
unsaved by sirens.

What is Right?

So long since I have written
the words not right

the feelings are too dormant
I cannot write

and when a word starts growing
it's just not right

because it is not glowing
I will not write

I dream of distant poems
I once could write.

The Gift of Ghazal

I'm knotted like a tree
so need a ghazal

thoughts collide inside
but not in ghazals

depression is my shawl
deep in the ghazal

writing with this weight
and words in ghazals

the music melts my heart
in songs of ghazals

so every day I write
the gift of ghazal.

Life Preserver

News is now a nightmare
I try to stay afloat

the government has lost its mind
I try to stay afloat

the virus kills a thousand more
I try to stay afloat

I take a walk to feel the sun
to try to stay afloat

or do pilates on my rug
to help me stay afloat

night time comes, the world's the same
no way to stay afloat

the life preserver broken now
nowhere left to float.

Hidden

One hundred children, sick, four dead
the sun goes into hiding

the virus spared them yesterday
the sun goes into hiding

each day I walk deserted streets
the sun, she still is hiding

children home, but scared to flee
the sun's gone into hiding

the world tips back, the clouds they cry
the sun's gone into hiding

scared to have my children die
the sun forever hiding.

Cradle in my Arms

Six months ago I saw my kids
and cradled them in arms,

the world had wings with which to fly
and cradle in my arms,

now the beaches close their doors
can't cradle in my arms

the parks are mourning swingless swings
to cradle in one's arms

today I dream of better days
to cradle in my arms

to see my babies close enough
to cradle in my arms.

The World Shut Down Its Hugs

Three months ago corona struck
the world shut down its hugs

the edict is six feet apart
the world shut down its hugs

everyone must wear a mask
the world shut down its hugs

even if you're lonely
the world shut down its hugs

I gaze longingly at grandkids
I'm not allowed to hug

it's social isolation
a world without its hugs

and mental hibernation
the world shut down its hugs.

With No Vaccine

Years before we hug
with no vaccine

I gaze at empty hands
with no vaccine

my smile disappears
with no vaccine

the mask fills up my face
with no vaccine

the absence of your touch
with no vaccine

it almost feels too much
with no vaccine.

A Mother's Lament

In memory of George Floyd

Each time he walks the street
he could be killed

Aubrey sought to run
and he was killed

George Floyd cashed a check
he soon was killed

he cried out to his Mama
then was killed

the color of his face
he could be killed

even if he's ten
he could be killed

Trayvon wore a hoodie
and he was killed

how does Mama sleep
when he is killed.

He Called for Mama

In Memory of George Floyd

Eight minutes on his chest
he called for Mama

now George Floyd is dead
he called for Mama

in heaven now with God
and also Mama

Black boys still harassed
without their Mama

children they are bruised
without their Mamas

while others in their graves
with tears of Mamas.

Police Shootings June, 2020

The boy just wants to walk
the world festers and it bleeds

Trayvon he took that walk
the world festers and it bleeds

Eric took a stroll
the world festers and it bleeds

Michael walked away
the world festers and it bleeds

Brenda went to sleep
the world festers and it bleeds

Ahmaud his daily run
the world festers and it bleeds

George went to the store
the world festers and it bleeds

the man just wants to breathe
festers, blood, death.

Thriving

I thought it would be over
the virus thrives

the president is maskless
the virus thrives

he says let's end insurance
the virus thrives

the children all are school less
the virus thrives

I look for hopeful signs
the virus thrives

Democracy is blind
the virus thrives.

Rage

I have friends, but still feel lonely
I watch the virus rage

now the world is filled with masks
I watch the virus rage

Texas now the new New York
I watch the virus rage

people live inside their cages
I watch the virus rage

are we the virus, all the lonely
who join the virus' rage

face and feelings covered blindly
the virus goes on rage.

News of News

The sunshine is my blanket
thrown off with news

I cherish my grandbabies
but still the news

the channel is now off
thrown off with news

they say live in the moment
filled with bad news

tomorrow is a new day
discard the news

at night sleep is a nightmare
with news of news.

Facetime with Ella

Every day at 5 o clock
I have facetime with Ella

Ella fills the screen with awe
her daily call from facetime

sometimes she interrupts my plans
I miss her call from facetime

without the hugs, without her breath
but still I have the facetime

I ask to see her brother Jake
she wants to hog the facetime

look forward to the time when there
is no call from facetime

when I embrace their face in flesh
and say goodbye to facetime.

Prayers 11: To Samantha Rose for her 30th

Born as breath
hands clasped in prayer like a rose

they placed a pink hat-a girl-a surprise
answer to prayers, named you Rose

explorer's eyes, but words that were few
what secret prayers in the rose of you

searching for snails, for magic, for flowers
the roses raised in prayer, all blue

your stalk, not tall, but a mind measured
by bouquets of colored roses

engrossed in anatomy, the stamen, the pollen
and prayers of fragrant roses

family first, with bursts and hibernations
dreams and desires that rose

dancing inside abundant gardens
passionate prayer, a Rose that grew.

Shared Room: A ghazal

To Elissa

You sixteen and me eighteen
we shared a room

college and its chaos
inside our room

graduation, a job, a wedding
in bigger rooms

after came the babies
no longer room

for reams of conversation
or quiet rooms

marriage, sometimes children
found us in ruins

secrets kept in vaults
locked in a room

again, we open house
to our heart's ruin

today another sorrow
invades our room

together we can climb
in our shared room.

Verbal Gymnastics

To Gregory Crosby, author of Said No One Ever

Such mental acrobatics
language leaping off the page

and diction that's dramatic
language leaping off the page

such specimens of beauty
language leaping off the page

it's his poetic duty
language leaping off the page

sentiments that make me cry
language leaping off the page

intellect that's running high
language leaping off the page

this poet is so deeply smart
language leaping off the page

he comprehends a broken heart
language weeping off the page.

Hands

To Ira

Married many years
we still hold hands

the tree I call your body
has many hands

you talk about your dreams
dealt a wrong hand

excavations and exploring
not in your hands

the husband and the father
such helpful hands

the depth of your desire
in my heart's hand.

Stuck Inside With You

My world has grown extremely small
stuck inside with you

to walk to cross a tiny bridge
stuck inside with you

news becomes a dance of death
stuck inside with you

changing channels frequently
stuck inside with you

movie theaters in the house
stuck inside with you

eating dinner, shared by two
stuck inside with you

days grow into weeks, then months
stuck inside with you

you bring a smile to my lips
unstuck because of you.

My heart, my ghazal

What else is there to write
aside from ghazals

you're always by my side
just like a ghazal

you give me words to weep
like grief in ghazals

there's talk, an endless treat
as in a ghazal

I've lived with you so long
you are my ghazal

I've shared my silly songs
and endless ghazals

you've always been my friend
so like a ghazal

I'll love you to the end
my heart, my ghazal.

Birthday Poem

To Ira, 68

Yesterday a storm exploded
and you were by my side

political unrest grown sour
but you were by my side

glass was broken every hour
you were by my side

the world is not the one I knew
still you are at my side

the politics it has me blue
yet you are by my side

the sun wakes up its palsied face
you still stay at my side

the day limps by, the virus race
and you are at my side

sometimes I dream a better place
you always by my side

how could I live without your grace?
without you by my side.

End of the Semester

To my City College Students, December, 2020

Teaching how to write
on screen with Zoom

words get warped of meaning
on screen with Zoom

students hide their faces
on screen with Zoom

stories still unfolding
on screen with Zoom

much mental unloading
on screen with Zoom

today the class is over
on screen with Zoom

I stare at empty boxes
of faceless Zoom.

Back to School

September comes, the sun she hides
the kids go back to school

a time to run and jump and slide
the kids go back to school

they now wear masks and sanitize
the kids go back to school

in class they sit, they cannot move
the kids go back to school

cannot hug their favorite friends
the kids go back to school

nor see some smiles with the mask
while sitting sad in school.

The New Normal

September is when school starts
my body bursts

to see all of my students
my body bursts

the classroom in my stage
my body bursts

technology my rage
my body bursts

now I teach on Zoom
my body bursts

with cameras that don't work
my body bursts

and tears that I can't see
my body bursts

and fears that can not flee
my body bursts

they say this is the new normal
my body bursts

to stare at empty screens
my body bursts.

Blind Black Box

I need to see your face
more than a black box

I want to see your smile
more than a black box

the tears scream and stream
upon this black box

talk becomes a task
hide in this black box

staying in the shadow
behind the black box

when will life return
not blind in a black box?

Sighs and Cries

December is about to start
the winter sighs and cries

the virus spreads in every heart
the winter sighs and cries

months of cold, no one outside
the winter sighs and cries

the holidays decide to hide
the winter sighs and cries

children learn in front of screens
the winter sighs and cries

we're living in a plague of mean
the winter sighs and cries.

Election, 2020

A new president is coming
the ghost he haunts the street

the government is splintered raw
the ghost he haunts the streets

protests swirl with guns and knives
the ghosts he haunts the streets

shouts of fraud, none in sight
the ghost he haunts the streets

proud boys march their Nazi swag
the ghost he haunts the streets

a governor is almost killed
the ghost he haunts the streets.

The Virus Rages

Today they stormed the capital
the virus rages

screams of "Hang Mike Pence"
the virus rages

sweatshirts signed "Camp Auschwitz"
the virus rages

smear the walls with excrement
the virus rages

maskless senators they hide
the virus rages

five people already died
the virus rages

guns are raised, a sign of power
the virus rages

grief keeps growing, rampant shower
the virus rages.

Vaccine, 2021

You stuck me in the arm
should I feel safe?

They say this should protect me
and keep me safe

no more coronavirus soon
I think I'm safe

yet people dying daily
I don't feel safe

a new president is coming
I dream of safe

the world right now so broken
I beg for safe.

Poetry Outreach, 2021

Last year we had a festival
words went wild

poetry was king and queen
words went wild

five year olds like flowers read
words so wild

poetry in language
of words and wild;

now we hibernate at home
words that whisper

we're muted into silence
in words that whisper

when can words come out again
outside the whisper

words, unsheltered
wild, unwhispered.

ABOUT THE AUTHOR

Pamela L. Laskin is a lecturer in the English Department at City College, where she teaches undergraduate and graduate Children's Writing, and directs the Poetry Outreach Center. Several of her children's and poetry books have been published. *Ronit and Jamil*, A Palestinian/Israeli *Romeo and Juliet* in verse was published by Harper Collins in 2017, and was named among the 35 books to have on your radar for 2017. *Bea*, a picture book, was a finalist for the Katherine Paterson Prize for Children's Fiction in 2018. She is the winner of the 2018 International Fiction Prize from Leapfrog Press, and *Why No Bhine*, an epistolary novel about the Rohingya Muslims, was published in 2019. The Operating System published a bilingual picture book, *Monster Maria*, which is about Hurricane Maria, and is being used as a fundraiser for after-school programs in Puerto Rico. Linus Press published *My Secret Wish* about families seeking asylum, and is also being used as a fundraiser for Immigrant Families Together.

The Lost Language of Crazy, a middle grade-novel, was published in November, 2021 (Atmosphere Press). She is currently at work with Ukrainian author Vasyl Makhno on a YA novel in verse, *Wisteria and Weeds*, whose focus is on the war in the Ukraine, and what it means for the lives of teens.

Finally, she is this year's (2023) recipient of Judith's Room Freedom Through Literacy Board option prize for her current novel.

Follow her: twitter@RonitandJamil and follow her blog: http://PamelaLaskin.blogspot.com

www.ingramcontent.com/pod-product-compliance
Lightning Source LLC
Chambersburg PA
CBHW021027090426
42738CB00007B/931